What Rea...

MW00611502

"I loved everything about this study! I didn't know much about Mary Magdalene before I started this study, but Emily quickly drew me into Mary's life, her character, her flaws and her special place in the life of Jesus. The study is full of challenging, thought-provoking questions that weaves Mary's life into the reader's current-day issues and experiences. The study is also full of historical commentary that was very informative and helped me become more aware of all that Mary probably experienced in life before she met Jesus and after she started following him. This study is great for a group Bible study or individual time of reflection. I look forward to more studies from this author!"

~Sharon S

"I absolutely loved this study. I found myself flipping through my Bible as I read along in the study. I really appreciate when questions are asked throughout the study because it helps keep me engaged and my thoughts flowing. That was the format for 'He Calls Us by Name,' and it was so helpful for me. I appreciate how the study allows for you to really explore and spend time in it but also allows for you to go through it quickly if needed. I loved the correlations from Mary's life and how that can relate to our own life. It is a great reminder to keep my eyes focused on Jesus and to wait for Him."

~Emily B

"The aspect I loved about the study, 'He Calls Us by Name,' was that it brought to life a woman in the Bible who is often skipped or overlooked in other studies but is a powerful testimony to the healing power of Jesus in the life of Mary Magdalene. The study provided historical and Biblical references as well as questions for study and personal reflection to further my walk with Christ. I would highly recommend this study to women and loved that the daily chapters were short and easy to fit into a busy schedule!"

~Ruthie S

"I very much enjoyed this study on Mary in 'He Calls Us By Name.' The entire study was really timely for me, and each day of the study, I was reminded of God's faithfulness to His people and encouraged to remain faithful in my current season of life. I highly recommend this study to all women!"

~Kylee M

"He Calls Us by Name' takes one of the most popular Bible stories, but breaks it into small chunks that allow you to see parts you didn't notice before. Historical facts from that time period helped me to better understand Mary on a more personal level. The setup allows for flexibility, so some days I spent a quick 10 minutes, other days when I had more time I spent 30 minutes. The open-ended questions allow for good discussions for a group or individual reflection. A great study for women in all walks of their faith."

~Carolyn G

He Calls Us by

Name

A Bible study on discovering how Mary Magdalene's story can inspire us to listen for Jesus' voice

Written by Emily Saxe

He Calls Us by Name

A Bible study on discovering how Mary Magdalene's
story can inspire us to listen for Jesus' voice

© 2019 Emily Saxe

ISBN 978-1-7342582-0-2

To all the women who feel less than, not enough and "just" ordinary. You don't need to be enough. Jesus is enough in your place and still desires your heart.

To Mary. One day, we'll meet in Heaven, and I apologize in advance for the many questions I will ask you!

Table of Contents

About this Study

*D*ear friend,

How excited I am for you to join me in studying the life of a woman I have grown to love and respect: Mary Magdalene. I became intrigued by Mary, who is only mentioned in the Bible by name 14 times, when I heard a short lesson on how Jesus appeared to her first out of anyone else on earth after He rose from the dead. And when He appeared to her, she didn't recognize Him until He spoke her name. I get goosebumps when I think about this moment. When Mary heard Jesus call her by name, and her eyes were opened.

It's my prayer for your eyes to be opened as you make your way through this Bible study. We are about to embark on a four-week journey together where we will take an honest look at how to strip away the things that distract us from keeping our eyes on Jesus and our ears ready to hear His voice calling us by name. Each day, we will look at a few different Scripture passages and answer questions not only about the context of that Scripture, but about how we can apply it to our own hearts and lives. You'll also have space for reflection and prayer at the end of each day. I must point out, though, that while this is a study on Mary, we will spend much of the first week in other areas of the Bible. We don't have much context for Mary's life before Jesus, so we will be setting the scene to prepare our hearts and minds for when Mary steps up in faithfulness.

I am filled with excitement at the thought of you opening your Bible, poising your pen and preparing your heart to study this woman who gave everything for Jesus. She wasn't perfect, and she certainly had to overcome insecurities and temptations, but that's one of the things I love about her. That she had to fight, just like we do today, to hear God call out to her and discern how to step through the open door of His purpose.

He calls us all by name. Are you ready to hear His voice?

–Emily

He will
lift us up
in His
truth

Week 1 🌹 Day 1

Intro Mary

*I*magine living in a time and place where you feel danger lurking around every corner. Your family and normal life in general are ruled by a government beyond your control. A government that hates you and your people. There is little stability in your life, and you wake up each morning wondering if you'll survive the day.

This was normal for many Jewish people living in the time of Jesus. The Romans had taken control, threatening their safety. Each day, they faced a harsh reality: Life could be easily taken from them at any moment. This is where Mary Magdalene's story starts.

This was life before Jesus.

Before we dive into the study of Mary Magdalene, I need to be honest with you about something: Very little is actually known about her. The Gospel writers only mention her name 14 times throughout the entire account of Jesus' life. But I don't believe that means we can take her for granted.

Quite the opposite, actually. Mary was a woman whose life points to the truth of the freedom we can have in Jesus. She reminds us of the strength that is ours when we put our trust in our Savior.

But before we can study this amazing woman, let's put to rest some rumors and confusion about her. She was a woman whose character has been slandered across the history books as a prostitute and mistress of Jesus. She is often confused with other Marys from Scripture. So let's point out from the start these misconceptions.

The most common misunderstanding is about her character. She has been accused of sinful actions based on where she was from and the fact that Jesus drove seven demons from her. Some believe she was a prostitute before she began following Jesus, or they assume her life was tainted by sexual sin. But there is no biblical or historical evidence connecting Mary to prostitution. Pop culture, through books and movies that have dramatized their relationship, has tried to make Mary Jesus' mistress and even His wife. But that's unfounded and entirely fiction. It breaks my heart how this woman's character has been dragged through the mud for the sake of a little drama.

Read 1 John 4:1-6

Why must we "test the spirits"?

Knowing the lies people have spread about Mary, how does this passage speak as a warning about listening to those lies without testing them against the truth?

What confidence can we have as we test the spirits?

So here's what we do know. She came from a town called Magdala, hence the "Magdalene." While the Bible says nothing of her home life or family, she most likely had no husband. Demons—seven of them, to be exact—took over her life and body for a time. She became a follower of Jesus and supported His ministry financially, although we don't know exactly from where her resources came. She was strong in character and faithfulness, as she was one of only a few of Jesus' followers who remained at the cross, watching Him die before her eyes. And, perhaps most notable, she was the first person to see and speak to the risen Christ, the very first to carry the good news.

OK, that's a lot of context! Each day of this study will not have that much reading and setting the scene, but I wanted to make sure we were all on the same page. I hope that clarifies a few things for you and excites you to keep on digging into Mary's world.

Read through 1 John 4:1-6 again. Also read James 4:4-10. Take time to pray through and journal in the space provided on the next page your thoughts on recognizing the Spirit of truth versus the spirit of falsehood. For the next four weeks, we will be hitting on topics about the truth of Jesus calling you, desiring you and using you. These are things Satan does not want you to hear. He may try to confuse you with the spirit of falsehood. Pray for the strength to resist the devil and remain humble before the Lord.

For He will lift us up in His truth.

Reflection

Day 2

Our Past Does Not Define Us

*A*s we continue setting the scene and getting to know who Mary was and who she wasn't, it's easy to grow frustrated with the lack of details surrounding her life. We don't know about her family, about the details of her life in Magdala or how she became the host for seven demons.

It's easy to look at everything we don't know and wonder why God wouldn't clue us in to more of her past. But maybe there's a reason for that. Maybe God wants us to understand how Mary's past does not define her.

And neither does yours.

We can pour over all 14 times Mary's name is mentioned in the Bible. (And we will over these four weeks!) We can look up historical documents to try and figure out what her life was like. But maybe God desires us to look beyond Mary's past. Maybe He wants us to know we don't need to dwell on, identify with or define ourselves by our pasts.

Mary was a woman who served Jesus with all her heart regardless of her past. Jesus wants you to do the same. You see, people have made up stories and horrible lies about Mary. All assumptions based on where she came from and the fact that she had seven demons living within her.

But regardless of her past, Jesus used her. He uses you, too.

Read Ephesians 2:1-3.

What does our past look like?

> *Magdala was a fishing town on the northwestern shore of the Sea of Galilee. It became known for its luxury and rough people who lived there.[1]*

What is this wrath we deserve?

It can be extremely difficult to think through the fact that we were followers of Satan before followers of Jesus. Especially if you've grown up in a Christian home and have known Jesus since you were little. I accepted Christ at the age of 5, so I know how passages like this one can almost feel like I'm excluded from experiencing the fullness of God's grace.

But regardless of how old you were when you found Christ, this life of death and following Satan was our fate before Jesus. This was Mary's fate before Jesus.

Praise God the story doesn't end there!

Read Ephesians 2:4–10

"Grace" is mentioned three times in this passage. Look up a definition of grace and write it below.

What do we have instead of death because of grace?

What was God's motivation for saving us (don't just write down the verse as your answer!)?

Jesus does not care about our past. Yes, He cares in the sense of wanting to heal our wounds and use everything for His glory. But He does not care in the sense that who we are before Him will never stop Him from calling our names.

We are alive because of what Jesus accomplished on the cross. We have a new identity in Christ, and we don't have to worry about our pasts defining us.

What do you currently allow to define who you are?

How does not knowing Mary's past encourage you in regards to your own past or your own sinful choices? (Use the top of the next page for more space as needed.)

Use the space below to reflect on God's grace making you alive in Christ. Read 1 Corinthians 1:26-31 for further encouragement and reflection.

Reflection

Day 3

The Changes of Sin

J have an extremely active imagination. Which means horror movies and I don't get along. In fact, I've been known to literally cover my eyes in the movie theatre when a horror movie trailer comes on the screen. Part of the reason I don't like those kinds of movies, though, is that I truly believe Satan has numbed our culture to the truth of his existence. If people enjoy watching scary truths like demon possession, then maybe they will start to think he and his henchmen are just created by Hollywood.

But demons are real. Demonic activity happens. Just ask Mary.

Seven demons possessed Mary. We read about it in Luke 8:2.

"...Mary (called Magdalene) from whom seven demons had come out..."

Seven often signified completeness. Some have wondered if the suffering she experienced from one demon was simply "complete" throughout her body. The number does not change her story, and I don't think it necessary to worry about that detail.

Her life was not a movie. The panic we experience when that adrenaline hits at the theatre wasn't created on set. It was her life. We don't know the details of what the demons actually did to her or caused her to do, but demon possession is demon possession, no matter how you look at it. She was a pawn of Satan.

This part of Mary's past is not meant to scare you and create worry about demon possession in your own life. I believe if you have accepted Jesus as your Savior and have the Holy Spirit living inside you, then demons cannot possess you. The Holy Spirit protects you, guards you and gives you power over demons.

So keep in mind as you read this that you are free in Christ.

During Mary's time, demon possession was not uncommon. But the people in that day believed in order for a demon to possess you, you had to allow that to happen by willingly sinning. Others believed those possessed were merely victims of the demon. [2]

While the Bible does not explicitly state "a demon will never possess a believer," there are many scriptures that support the concept. 1 John 5:18, Colossians 1:13 and 2 Corinthians 6:15 point to this.

Whatever the specifics of their beliefs, everyone thought those possessed were unclean. This means Mary could not go to a place of worship. She could not even have contact with many people, as it was also believed you could catch a demon.

She was an outcast. Living a life of shame, she might have even been ostracized from her family and community. And she was chained to the will of Satan.

Read Jude. (Don't freak out about reading an entire book of the Bible in one sitting—it's only 25 verses!)

What had sin done to the ungodly people about whom Jude wrote?

These are people who mask as believers, which means many of them might have truly claimed Christ as Savior. How, though, had their sin changed them from claiming Christ to actually following Satan?

Our sin changes us. It separates us from those we love. Mary most likely could not live with her family unless, of course, they chose to not ostracize her. But even then. Imagine a friend or family member who lived at the whims of the devil. True, Mary could not control when those demons took over, but they most definitely changed her mind, her words, her actions.

I can only imagine how scared she must have been. How isolated she must have felt. But I'm guessing, as we look more at her strength and courage later on in her life, that she learned quite a bit about fighting back and standing up against temptation.

For God can use even the worst of circumstances to grow us into mighty warriors.

Look toward the end of Jude at his call to persevere. We, unlike Mary at the time of her possession, have the Holy Spirit dwelling within us. And we can take a stand against the devil.

How do we build ourselves up in the most holy faith?

What are ways you still stumble daily?

There are many people in our lives like Mary: Those who are controlled by sin. Some are allowing it, others do not realize how much Satan controls them. What challenge does Jude give in regards to these people?

Read 1 Corinthians 6:9–11

Use the space below to reflect on how Jesus' death on the cross has freed you from the punishment we all deserve.

Reflection

Day 4

Getting Rid of Distraction

Yesterday we learned about Mary's possession and what that might have meant in her life. Reading about the history or different Bible verses regarding demon possession, it can feel somewhat far off and withdrawn from reality. But there is a spiritual war going on right this very moment.

This battle between good and evil happens all around us, mostly without our realizing it. I know for me, that is a difficult concept to grasp. And a scary one, too. We must all gain a healthy understanding that Satan's purpose is to distract us and cause us to turn from God as much as possible.

He's real, he's our enemy, and he seeks to destroy us (read 1 Peter 5:8 to see how he's described).

We might not have actual demons dwelling within us, but we do have things in our lives that distract us from following Jesus with all our hearts. Mary's physical body and mind were overtaken by seven demons. What has overtaken you?

What has Satan used to make you as ineffective for God as possible?

What has distracted you from God most recently? This could literally be anything from comparing yourself to that perfect-looking woman to dwelling on sinful thoughts to ... literally anything.

Read James 1:13-15

What truth about temptation do you see in these verses?

What aspects of God's character do you learn about here?

Keep in mind, when you allow sin to distract you from God, that doesn't just affect you. It also affects those in your life. Think about Mary's possession. She was most likely unable to love, support and encourage the people in her life. Her demon possession didn't just affect her own routine. The people she spent time with each day had to deal with her demons, too. Not in the same completeness, but I'm sure they hurt as they watched her struggle and tried to help her.

Our sin affects our loved ones. The truth that our sin breaks God's heart should be enough to stop us in our tracks, but sometimes it's a needed reminder that our decisions affect the humans in our lives, too.

But we don't have to let those distractions drag us away and give birth to sin.

Read Colossians 3:1-3

What does it mean, beyond the promise of eternal life, to be raised with Christ?

What does it mean to set your mind on things above?

We must begin living with an eternal perspective. When we set our minds on things above, we hold the day-to-day loosely, knowing God is in control of all things. We begin to think about things for what they mean in light of eternity.

When Satan tries to distract us with plans falling through or sickness or an argument with a friend, we can think about it all in the context of eternity.

Does that plan *really* matter in regards to furthering God's kingdom?

Will I chose to remember my body will waste away but my soul lasts forever?

How can I restore peace with my friend knowing her soul holds more importance than my hurt?

How have the distractions in your life kept you from experiencing the fullness of God?

What will you do, right now, to fight against those distractions that desire to drag you away and entice you into sin?

Reflect below after reading Romans 8:1-11 about the freedom you have in Christ.

Reflection

Day 5

It's Time to Stand Firm

We've come to the end of Week 1. It might feel like we've done a lot of talking about things that don't involve Mary, and, honestly, that's because we just don't have much context for her life. But we can use these Scriptural findings we've been studying to help us form a better picture of what life might have been like for her. And how we can take a stand against our own sinful pasts.

We all have ways we allow our sin nature to creep along the path to idol status in our hearts. There's simply no getting around it until we leave our flesh behind us for our new, heavenly bodies. We can, however, work at keeping an eternal perspective and remaining open to the conviction of the Holy Spirit. We can learn how to recognize the devil's schemes and call upon the Name of Jesus for strength to resist the temptation of turning our minds toward an earthly perspective.

For Jesus desires to help us.

Read Philippians 4:4–9

Without simply listing what Paul tells us to think on, what are ways to set your mind on things above?

What promise does God give to us, and how does that encourage you as you take a stand against your sin?

If we're to take seriously our new identity in Christ, if we truly desire to take a stand against the schemes of the devil, then we need to put passages like this one into serious practice. Make a habit of repeating these verses to yourself over and over again when you know there's a spiritual war going on for your attention.

This next passage we're going to read is most likely very familiar to you. So as you read through it, take the time to ask God to reveal something new to you. His Word is alive and active, and we will never get to a place where we're done learning, even with a passage like this one.

Ask God to reveal something new to you before reading.

Read Ephesians 6:10-18

What stood out to you as you read this familiar passage?

Which pieces of armor are difficult for you to wear? How can God's truth help you overcome those difficulties?

There is no armor to protect our back. Why do you think that is?

This armor is not a suggestion. It's not something we can pick and choose from when deciding what pieces of armor to wear. This is a command from God and our defense against Satan. This is how we are to live out our new identity.

Like Mary, though, others might look at our lives and decide how they will define us. Despite our faithfulness to Jesus, there are those who will look for ways to smear our names and create for us histories we never lived. In those moments, remember these passages. Remember to think on only what is true. Remember to pick up your armor with which you can stand firm in God's protection.

We cannot control what others say, but we can control how we choose to respond. So as Satan continues to fight a war against you and against the angels in the spiritual realm, will you pick up your armor and stand sure? Will you choose Jesus this day? Will you live in the identity He has given you, fighting against anything that distracts you?

Spend time in reflection about this past week and the things God revealed to you. Write down any questions you have so you can ask a wise friend or look up a trustworthy commentary. Then, write down your own prayer in the space provided.

Reflection

No sin
is beyond
His
forgiveness

Week 2 🌹 Day 1

Freedom

*I*magine seeing Jesus for the first time. I mean, literally seeing Him. What a moment of immeasurable joy! For those of us who have given our lives to Christ, that moment will prove beyond anything we can imagine.

But for those who have rejected Him, who have never accepted His forgiveness, that moment will most likely be one of sheer terror.

We don't have any indication of what it was like when Mary saw Jesus for the first time. She probably had heard of Him, since word traveled fast and her seashore town was most likely a place Jesus came to preach. It's easy to picture that moment of His releasing her from her demon chains as one of ultimate and final peace. But when we take a look at the Scriptures, we soon realize driving out demons was never a pretty sight.

Read Mark 1:21–28

Why did the demon admit Jesus' true identity?

What was the response of the demon at Jesus' command?

Read Mark 9:14-29

What was the physical result of this possession of a young boy?

What characteristics of Jesus are revealed here?

Read Luke 8:26-39

Why didn't the demons obey Jesus immediately?

What was the physical result of the demons leaving this man?

It doesn't take reading many of these true accounts to realize how demons did not leave their hosts peacefully. These are not calm, cool and collected events. So we can assume Mary's exorcism followed suit.

Here we see a picture of what it looks like to hand over our sin to Jesus. It's not pretty, and if we hold back, it can be awfully painful, too. Satan does not want you or me to allow Jesus to remove our sin from our minds and souls. He wants us to fight for our sin, to cling to it, to fall to the ground in protection of it.

But holding onto sin only leaves us with wounds and keeps us from truly experiencing Jesus.

Take a moment right now to pray through any sin you don't want Jesus to remove from your life. Pray for the strength to hand it over to Jesus right now.

You want to know one of the most beautiful aspects of every single demon-possession story? Jesus continued to pursue those held in Satan's grasp. He didn't let the demons talk Him out of freeing those caught in chains.

Whether or not Mary sought out Jesus or the other way around, Jesus chose to free Mary from her demons. He chose to free her from her past the instant He reached out and and said, "Be free."

Jesus pursues you in the mess of your sin. He pursues you even in the midst of that same sin you commit each day when you've promised yourself and God you wouldn't go back to it. He pursues you even when Satan fights against Him for your attention. And He pursues you even when you say no the first few times He approaches.

For no sin is beyond His forgiveness.

No attitude is beyond His restoring. No heartbreak is beyond His healing.

What about knowing that Jesus chose to free Mary from her demons encourages you? (Use top of next page for more space as needed.)

How can you live each day knowing Jesus pursues you even in the mess of your sin? Spend time reflecting on that, specifically for how you can live this week, and write your thoughts in the space below.

Reflection

Day 2

Choosing Jesus

$\mathcal{D}$o you remember the moment you gave your life to Jesus? Or a moment when you truly felt His presence sweeping through you? Those are moments you can't keep to yourself! When Jesus changes us, we must respond. We can't stay the same once Jesus sets us free.

Mary certainly couldn't.

Over the next few days, we'll study how Mary left her past behind her and entered into a new life of serving Jesus and the disciples. Luke 8:1-3 tells us of Mary's role in Jesus' ministry. For now, let's focus on the fact that Mary changed her life to follow Jesus after He freed her from her demons, something we know because of Luke 8.

When we go through dramatic events, we can't stay the same, even if we want to hold onto the past. We can't pretend things haven't changed, that we haven't changed. Mary couldn't either. And so she left her old life behind her and dedicated herself to Jesus.

This change can also be seen in another miraculous moment.

Read Luke 17:11-19

Why did the other nine not return to thank Jesus?

What characteristics do we see in the one who returned?

Like the man who threw himself at the feet of Jesus, Mary didn't receive her healing and flee to return to normal life. Because here's the thing: We don't have to accept our new identity. We can live a lie and attempt to go back to our old ways, assuming speaking words like, "Jesus, come into my heart and forgive me," mean we're covered in the blood of the Lamb.

But it's so much more than words. It's acceptance. It's new life.

Read 2 Corinthians 5:17

What is new when someone becomes a Christian and is a "new creation"?

What does this mean for our old life?

You've probably read this verse hundreds of times. What is something you notice right now in reading it in regards to God's character?

We must distance ourselves from our sin when Jesus frees us. We cannot attempt to live in our old life while at the same time squeezing into a new creation outfit. It just doesn't work like that.

Mary's response to the freedom Jesus gave her remains an example to this day of how we can — and should — respond to Jesus. Our hearts' desires should no longer wade in the waters of sin, believing we can have both Jesus and this world. We must humbly kneel at His feet, knowing this is what He came for and died for all those years ago. For us. For our hearts. For our lives.

So we must decide if we, like Mary, will walk forward in freedom, or if we will allow the demons of our sin to continue controlling us, unwilling to accept the forgiveness of the One who shed His blood for our freedom.

What will you choose this day? For even if we've made a decision to follow Jesus with our lives, it's still easy to slink back to our chains. Each day we must choose Jesus. Each day we must, like Mary, bask in the redemptive shadow of our Savior.

As you reflect today, read Romans 5:8 and write out your praise and any conviction you have about choosing Jesus over your sin.

Reflection

Day 3

I Have Decided

*A*s we dive into learning about Mary's role as one of Jesus' followers, we have to wrap our minds around what it was like for women in her day. Women were not treated as individuals. They were seen as part of a family unit, as mothers and wives. Essentially, women had the same rights as a slave.

But Jesus didn't care about the societal rules. He healed on the Sabbath, turned tables in the temple courts and yes, He had women as part of His close-knit group. So as Mary left her life behind her to follow Jesus, she not only had freedom from her demonic oppressors, but she also entered a new life that would have been unheard of in those days.

We can assume Mary had no husband, as she is called Mary Magdalene, not Mary insert husband's name here. But despite not having a husband, she still had to leave the comforts of home and whatever family and friends she had in Magdala. She had to journey with a group of men who might not have respected her at first. She had to leave everything she knew.

All because life with Jesus meant more to her than comfort.

> *Women were low in the social hierarchy. Many women were not permitted to talk to men who were not their husbands, even if these men were guests in their homes. According to some scholars, women also held no rights to earn an education. Not only that, but they were not even allowed to speak in public.*[3]

But the fear of the unknown did not stop her from following her Savior.

Read Philippians 3:7–11

Obviously Paul didn't think his life actual garbage (or rubbish or dung, depending on the translation). So what exactly did he mean?

> *While it wasn't uncommon for women to travel with entertainers, their role in those situations was more of concubine—a woman living with a man without being his wife—than follower.*[4]

What would Paul have considered gains?

What do you consider gains in your own life?

God does not call all of us to pack our bags and head to a different country or to live on the streets with the homeless. But He does ask something of us. He commands it, actually. He commands us to leave our sinful lives behind us and follow Him.

Mary knew leaving her sinful life behind her meant physically leaving. Paul knew for his own life, it meant spreading truth where he once spread hatred.

Even though leaving a life of sin will look different for us all, know there is action that must occur. Like we read about yesterday, we can't simply say a prayer and then expect everything to change. We must be willing to share what Jesus has done.

Imagine if Mary accepted the freedom Jesus provided but then stayed home, never sharing her redemption story with anyone? If her life didn't change, what would that say about her heart?

In what ways are you keeping your story to yourself?

What do you need to give up to follow Jesus more wholeheartedly?

Mary was not some superhuman, amazing woman who instantly gave up all she had and ran toward Jesus, hair and makeup perfect in the process. Her story is a messy one. She probably ached over leaving her old life behind her. She probably feared what the disciples would think of her. And she probably wondered if Jesus truly was whom He said He was.

But she went. She looked at her fears and decided following Jesus was more important than anything else.

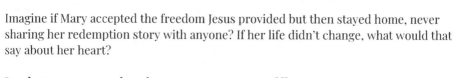 *Will you do the same today?*

Think about your dreams and desires right now. Then head back to Philippians and read that passage again. Many of us are not living in our sin, but rather we desire to follow Jesus with our lives. Take time to pray through your desires and ask God to reveal to you if your desires lean more toward this world or toward following Him.

Reflection

Day 4

Humble Servant

*C*aregiver. That's the title I've decided to bestow upon Mary. While in today's world we read that title and think caring for the sick, a caregiver helps with the daily needs of those in her life. Mary, along with a few other women, took on the responsibility of the behind-the-scenes work, the daily needs. While the disciples were on the frontlines with Jesus, Mary had a slightly different role.

Read Luke 8:1–3

What do you think Mary's role as caregiver entailed, based on this Scripture?

What characteristics must these women have had to carry out their roles in Jesus' ministry?

List some lies Mary might have believed about her role as caretaker/administrator. Then list out a truth to combat that lie. (For instance: Lie — Jesus doesn't think I'm capable of doing anything but preparing food. Truth — Jesus has given me a job to do, and He has entrusted it to me.)

It's funny how we don't really think about the fact that when Jesus and His disciples weren't out on the hillside teaching or in the town ministering to people, they were...somewhere. They had to sleep, to eat, to relax.

Maybe we don't think about those things because Jesus was, well, Jesus. He could speak food into existence. Why would He need Mary to help with that? Which is a characteristic of Jesus that proves beautiful: He doesn't need us, yet He wants us.

Jesus did not need Mary or the other women to provide for Him and His disciples. He could have easily provided for each and every need. But He allowed them to serve Him and do their part in His ministry.

You see, Mary wasn't just following Jesus to get something from Him. She didn't cling to His side, wanting Him to make her feel good about her life, wanting Him to make her life easy. She followed Him to serve. She believed He was who He said He was. And she wanted to be a part of that in any way possible.

How do we see Mary's humility here?

What could have easily held her back from serving Jesus?

What are the areas of your own life that are holding you back from serving Jesus? From giving instead of just taking?

Read Hebrews 12:1-3

Mary had eyes fixed on Jesus. Think about her past in the midst of her service. She might have felt like she had nothing to truly give Jesus. How could she, someone who once housed seven demons, minister to the King of Kings? How could she, a woman in the midst of many men, make an impact on those around her?

But Mary was a walking testimony of Jesus' power.

And now, she could be a living reminder of what it means to give one's life and serve with a humble heart. For each time the disciples looked at her, they could be reminded of all Jesus did for her. Each time she wondered her purpose of doing the mundane tasks of caring for the needs of these men, she could remind herself she was serving Jesus.

Her service, no matter how insignificant it might have felt, mattered. Your daily service, no matter how mundane it might feel, matters. It not only serves as a testimony to those around you of the power of Jesus at work in your life, but it also pleases your Savior. He has placed you exactly where He desires you to serve Him.

What sin might have entangled Mary during her time of serving Jesus and His disciples?

How does Mary's role as caretaker relate to your own area of current service?

What are ways Mary encourages you in the midst of your service?

What can you do each day to not grow weary or lose heart in the midst of mundane tasks and acts of service?

Spend time journaling below about how Mary's role as caretaker encourages you to use your own gifts and talents to serve God. In what ways are you doing so, and in what areas do you need to start serving?

Reflection

Day 5

Making a Difference

J want to take one more day to talk about Mary's service and dig a little deeper into what this meant for her. Yesterday I touched briefly on how Mary must have wondered how she could make a difference. And I think that is something we all have in common.

Has anyone ever told you you couldn't accomplish something? That you weren't smart enough, didn't have enough resources, weren't the right type? Or have you ever told yourself that? Have you ever whispered to yourself that you don't have what it takes? I know I have.

I'm not leading the charge on women's rights, but it can prove difficult to make a difference in a male-dominated world. Now imagine how Mary must have felt. Talk about a male-dominated world! Mary probably thought she had nothing to offer Jesus. Here He was, the One who had rescued her from her demons. The One who had fed 5,000 people from a scrap-of-a meal.

And *she* was supposed to minister to *Him*?

Mary must have looked at the band of men by Jesus' side, the ones who walked out the door with Him each day and came back in the evenings talking of all they saw and all they did. She must have wondered how she could ever compare to them.

But here's the thing. Mary didn't allow the social constraints of her day to hold her back from making a difference. We know her name, thousands of years later. We know her as one of the women who supported Jesus. Who remained faithful to Him.

Read Romans 12:1-8

We can get caught up in wanting to know God's specific will for our lives or how He wants to use us specifically. According to this passage, what does God desire of us in regard to His will?

How does God use us?

How does believing you are limited by your circumstances hold you back from serving Jesus?

How are you limiting yourself because of what you believe you are capable of doing for Jesus?

 *God adores your service.*

He loves how you use your gifts and talents to praise Him. Hear this truth: Even if there is never a single person who believes you are making a difference, know that God loves the way you serve Him.

Mary reminds us that God considers us worth it. It doesn't matter our social status, our talents or our past. He is pleased when we follow Him out of love and a desire to serve. No service is insignificant in His eyes.

Take time to reflect on why Mary's service and how she followed Jesus affects/encourages you to set aside any preconceived notions of what you're capable of doing for God.

Reflection

We are in
the hands
of
Jesus

Week 3 🌹 Day 1

A Living Nightmare

*W*hat is your worst fear? Something you don't even like to think about for fear it becoming reality. I imagine Mary's worst fears revolved around the building threats of the Pharisees. But even she could not foresee what was about to happen.

Mary was not present during Jesus' arrest. It's uncertain when exactly she joined the crowd of onlookers, but we know she certainly did join at some point. Which means someone had to come bang on her door and reveal the terrible news that Jesus was arrested.

It's the call nobody wants. The one telling you your worst fears are realized. Did Mary crumble to the floor? Did she scream out in anger at the unjustness of it all? Maybe. Whatever her initial response, she did not allow the fear of what might happen to stop her from running to Jesus.

This love, this dedication, this faithfulness brought her to the foot of the cross.

Read Mark 15:40-41 and Matthew 27:32-50

Why do you think Scripture points out the women present at Jesus' death?

What do you think kept Mary at the foot of the cross despite the horrid scene she witnessed? (Use top of next page for more space as needed.)

If you were Mary, what visuals would have burned their way into your memory? What words of Jesus would have done the same? Why?

Mary watched her Savior die. She never abandoned Him. Even in the face of not knowing what would happen next,

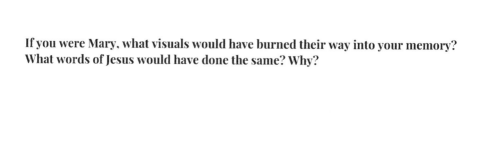

she remained.

What questions might Mary have struggled with while watching Jesus die?

How do you think Satan took advantage of Mary's questions at this moment?

Satan is never too busy to attempt to distract us from Jesus. Even with Jesus hanging on a tree, left for dead, Satan most likely crept his way into Mary's thoughts, causing her to doubt her Savior and question her loyalty.

I honestly don't know how she remained there, watching Jesus die. What horror that must have been for her. But we must remember Mary was only human. Which means God gave her the strength to remain on that hill.

He can give you strength, too. No matter what nightmare you face, no matter how weak you feel or how tempting it is to turn your face from reality, know God can provide you with the strength you need to stand firm. To stand firm and to stand tall.

Roman law forbid mourning for those who were being executed, which means the women were not allowed to grieve openly at the foot of the cross. [5]

We must pray for this strength and courage daily. Mary did not wake up that day and think, *Jesus will die this afternoon.* This caught her off guard. But the loyalty and love for Jesus running through her veins enabled her to face the cross even as Jesus' blood dripped from His dying body.

This love, this loyalty, is not something we see in Mary only to sigh and believe it's something unattainable for our own lives. Mary must have dealt with the desire to flee, giving into the temptation that most of the disciples gave into the night before the cross. But God, who is rich in mercy, gave her the strength to stand up under that temptation.

Read 1 Corinthians 10:12–13

What are your temptations right now?

How does God provide a way out of temptation for you?

Reflect in the space below and on the next page as needed about God giving Mary strength to remain at the foot of the cross and watch Jesus die. Replace any lies with the truth that you can have that same strength, no matter what you face.

Reflection

Day 2

Sitting in the Pain

*I*t wouldn't be fair to simply say God gives us strength without acknowledging just how debilitating our fears can be. Having courage does not mean we have no fear. Mary proved herself an immensely courageous woman by remaining at the cross. But her courage and loyalty do not mean lack of fear or sorrow.

While not diminishing the trials we have all gone through, Mary experienced one of the most horrific, nightmarish moments in all of history. Yet she stayed. She did not flee. It would have been easy for her to run and hide. People probably wouldn't have blamed her.

But if she had fled, she would have missed what happened next.

Read Matthew 27:51–56

What would Mary have missed witnessing if she had fled?

What impact do you think this moment had on her? In other words, what truth was revealed?

Sometimes God allows us to sit in our pain and experience sorrow in order to gain a better understanding of who He is. Mary most likely struggled against the fear that Jesus was not whom He said He was. She might have wondered if it had all been a lie. After all, if He truly was the Messiah, wouldn't He be able to come off that cross?

But when the land went dark, when the earth shook, God made His presence known. "Surely He was the Son of God!"

Whether or not Mary connected the dots in that moment, I want to reflect her courage in the face of fear. She looked to Jesus throughout each traumatic moment. I want to keep my eyes on Him, the author and perfecter of my faith, no matter what I go through in life.

But oh, how easy it is to take our eyes off of Jesus when fear strikes! We easily begin to form a battle plan in our minds. We look to our own solutions instead of to the cross. Instead of to the promise that Jesus can make beauty from ashes.

How do you allow your own fears to keep you from looking to Jesus?

What are your go-to solutions that don't include looking to Jesus?

Thinking about what Mary witnessed as she remained facing her fears and looking to Jesus, what promises do you know from Scripture that remind you God does all things for your good and His glory?

Tomorrow we will look into three different ways to look to Jesus in the midst of our routines. But for now,

Read 2 Timothy 1:7

How can you use the Spirit God has given you to fight against fears when worry or anxiety or trials come?

Reflect on the next page about times God has made beauty from ashes when you have kept your eyes on Him in the midst of fear. If you can't think of a time, reflect on what Mary experienced and how that encourages you for what you might face in the future.

Reflection

Day 3

Eyes on Jesus

*A*s promised, today we will look into three different ways to keep our eyes on Jesus instead of our fears. We'll focus on reading Scripture and answering questions as opposed to continuing on with Mary's story for now, so get your Bible ready and your pen poised.

 *Prayer*

We've all experienced moments of doubting Jesus in the midst of pain. Those moments don't have to mean we walk away from Him, but it's certainly common to question His methods or our circumstances. What will our next step be, though, in the midst of our doubt?

Read Matthew 14:22–33

Why did Peter doubt Jesus?

What was Jesus' response to Peter's doubt?

What did Peter do in the midst of his doubt?

How does this passage encourage you to pray in the midst of any doubt you experience?

We are in the hands of Jesus. He doesn't ask things of us only to let us slip through His fingers. Peter feared drowning, so he took his eyes off Jesus. But that didn't stop Jesus from reaching out and grabbing hold of him. May we all cry out to Jesus in prayer when we worry the waves of our troubles will crash us to our death.

How does prayer keep you focused on Jesus? Think of this practically, in the midst of your day-to-day. Go beyond the easy answer.

 *Humility*

The context of this passage is Peter speaking to the elders of the church. But that doesn't mean these characteristics are only for elders.

It's difficult to admit, but doubting Jesus and giving into fear means we believe we know better than God. When we doubt Him, we call Him untrustworthy. It takes humbling ourselves and admitting our pride to keep our eyes on Jesus.

Read 1 Peter 5:6–7

What does it mean that God will lift us up?

What happens when you cast your anxiety on God?

How do you change when you humble yourself?

There's no doubt in my mind that Mary questioned the circumstances before her as she stood at the foot of the cross. Doubt, fear, anger and more must have ripped their way through her thoughts and heart. But if things had gone differently that Friday afternoon, Jesus would not have overcome our sins and the devil. He would not have gained victory over the grave.

God knows what He's doing. He is in control and will work out all things for His glory. We just have to remain humble enough to watch Him work.

Memorize His promises

There is power in the Word of God. It's not called a double-edged sword for nothing. When we hide God's Word in our hearts, we grow in strength and protection against fear. We also hear the truth instead of the lies that threaten us to doubt. And we can respond accordingly.

Read Romans 8:38-39

What power do you see in this passage?

What characteristics of God do you see?

How would memorizing a verse like this help you keep your eyes on Jesus?

So what will you choose this day? Will you see the horror of your circumstances and run like the disciples? Or will you choose to keep your eyes on Jesus, remaining at the foot of the cross, like Mary? Obviously we all want to say we would stand firm like Mary. And we can start by putting these three points into practice each and every day.

Reflect on these three tips. Which one is most difficult for you and why? What scares you about remaining at the foot of the cross, and how can you find hope and encouragement in Jesus this day?

Reflection

Day 4

When God is Silent

*J*esus was dead. It was finished. The disciples were hiding. Mary and the other women were mourning. All was lost.

Read Matthew 27:57-61

Can you imagine what Saturday must have been like for Mary? Jesus had breathed His last with a great cry. His body was gently lifted from the cross and placed in a tomb. Mary probably wasn't slinking around watching. She most likely helped clean Jesus' body and bring Him to what she believed was His final resting place. How scarring that must have been.

Have you ever lost someone you love? The grief can feel unbearable. Like physical pain. And for Mary and all of Jesus' followers, they had to wait to mourn properly until Sunday. Saturday, their Sabbath, was not a day to mourn.

I wonder if Mary felt abandoned. Here she was, a woman who had given up all she had to follow this man who claimed to be the Messiah. But yet He died. Did she cry out to God, asking why He had abandoned them all?

Sometimes it seems as if God is silent. But even in the midst of questioning and grieving and wondering if God hears us, we can have hope.

Read Isaiah 43:1-3

What is the overall theme of this passage?

Why do we not need to fear?

Are there areas in your life right now where God seems silent? Which areas?

How can you find hope in the midst of what you are experiencing based on this passage?

Think about the ramifications of Jesus' death for Mary and the other disciples. They had spent years following Him, putting their hope in believing He would deliver them from the Romans. Had they been following a fraud? Did God actually not care what happened to them? Or even worse, did God break His promises regarding the coming Messiah?

They must have felt like all hope was lost.

But we know Who awaited them the next day.

What would have been the purpose of this Sabbath day for Mary? How could God have used this day for His glory?

It must have been easy for Mary to lose all hope. Knowing what you know, what would you say to Mary if you could speak to her on this day?

We know the full picture, but Mary didn't at the time. Reflect on your own circumstances or something that has happened in your life that you don't understand. God sees the full picture even when we don't. How will you take your own advice from the previous question? Reflect on the next page.

Reflection

Day 5

Day of Reflection

*T*ake this day to be still before God. Mary had to wait 24 hours before heading to the tomb. She spent that time most likely in emotional turmoil. But you don't have to do the same. Sometimes it seems like God's not there, that there is no hope. But He is always there. Come before Him with your fears and doubts today. Use the Scripture listed below to guide you in your time, but don't feel obligated to look up each one. There is space provided if you desire to write out any prayer or reflection.

Deuteronomy 31:8

Psalm 27:1-3

Psalm 30

Psalm 46:1-3

Psalm 73:26

2 Corinthians 12:9-10

Philippians 4:6

Colossians 1:13

2 Thessalonians 3:3

2 Timothy 4:17

Jesus doesn't
need us,
but He
wants us

Week 4 🌹 Day 1

He is Not Here

$\mathcal{S}$unday at dawn. The moment the Sabbath was over, Mary and her friends were rushing out to gather spices to anoint Jesus' body. Let me paint a picture of what this meant for these women. Probably exhausted from lack of sleep, they headed out as the sun just began to shed light over the earth. Women walking alone in the near-dark would have been dangerous. Not only that, but they knew Roman guards awaited them.

Knowing where Jesus was buried from witnessing His dead body being laid to rest, the women headed out in the direction of the tomb. They knew they were about to look into the face of their dead Savior.

Read Matthew 28:1-10 and Mark 16:1-8 (Luke 24:1-12 also has the account)

What do you think Mary was thinking and feeling as she headed to the tomb?

What drove her to walk to the tomb in the midst of exhaustion and danger?

The process of embalming and anointing a dead body was a sign of honor in those days. The more spices and ointment used, the higher respect paid.[6]

When reading the different Gospel accounts of this morning, it can be easy to grow confused at the timeline of events. We must remember to look at Scripture as a whole and that each Gospel writer was speaking to a different audience and therefore highlighted different moments.

Based on what the angel said to them, what do you think were the reactions of the women when they entered the tomb?

I can only imagine how confusing this moment must have been for these women. We read the angel's words and immediately understand what he means. Jesus is alive! He has risen from the grave and conquered death! We are saved from our sins!

But remember, these women had no context except for Jesus' teaching and Old Testament prophecies. They had mourned in agony for the past two days. And now, on this third day, they had come to honor the dead. But this terrifying being told them what?

Jesus was not there!

We know about Mary's confusion from John 20:2 when she runs to Peter and John saying, "They have taken the Lord out of the tomb, and we don't know where they have put him!" The angel had told her to go and tell Jesus' disciples where to meet Him. But what did Mary do instead?

Why would Mary have not believed the angel's words?

What fears must have gripped her as she ran to tell the disciples what she had seen and heard? (Use top of next page for more space as needed.)

How have you doubted, like Mary, the truth of what God has done in your life? What has made you doubt?

I can't blame Mary too much for doubting. She had seen Jesus die with her own eyes. She had watched as Joseph placed Him in a tomb. Now, His body was gone. Was she really supposed to believe in the impossible?

But even in this doubt, God used Mary. Remember, women during the time of Mary were not high on the society chain. They were not allowed to speak in public. Their word would not be taken as truth. Yet God chose Mary as the one to share this message.

What is significant about the fact that God used a woman to bear testimony to His resurrection?

God's plans are far more intricate than we realize. What does this tell you about the way He can use you?

Mary obeyed the angel in the face of her fear and doubt. She allowed God to use her even though she didn't fully understand. What are ways you can obey God right now, even if you don't see the full picture of what He is doing?

Reflect over the passages from today and over Mary's faithfulness, doubt and obedience. Remember, Mary wasn't superwoman. She was flesh and blood like you and me. She felt fear and unworthiness. She questioned God's plans. How, then, do her actions encourage you today?

Reflection

Day 2

"Mary"

$\mathcal{T}$oday we will study my absolute favorite part of Mary's story. But before we get there, let's set the scene.

Read John 20:1-15

What was Mary's response in the midst of all this news she was hearing?

How did her emotions cloud her sight of the truth?

Mary allowed her fear, unbelief and sorrow to mask the truth. The truth that stood right before her very eyes! I chuckle when I think about how Peter and John saw the empty tomb but then returned to where they were staying. Mary, on the other hand, stayed at the tomb and wept.

Can you picture that exchange between these men who saw the fact that Jesus was no longer in the tomb and Mary who wanted to remain to have a private moment to weep? Some things between men and women never change!

Regardless of how that conversation happened, I can't help but notice how Mary placed her belief in her emotions over the truth. This was not a perfect woman. She allowed her fears and her sadness to block out the voice of Jesus.

How have you allowed your emotions to block out the truth? What truths have you missed out on because of your fear or whatever emotion controlled you?

Read Mary's response to Jesus in verse 15. What does that tell you about Mary's character and drive, despite her fear?

Mary's response also makes me stop and wonder what she was possibly thinking. Here she was, a woman in hysterics, and she wanted to go off on her own and find a dead body to do ... what with it? Sling Jesus over her shoulder and carry Him back to the tomb? But this tells me she was still that dedicated to Jesus. She was willing to risk her safety to ensure Jesus' body was unharmed and not dishonored.

In the midst of all this, Mary literally was speaking to the One for whom she searched. She was seeing Jesus, but not perceiving Him. She was speaking to Him, but not understanding.

Why do you think Mary did not recognize Jesus?

> The original Greek word used to describe Mary here means she saw but did not perceive. To perceive means to become aware of something, and to understand and realize what it is you see.[7]

What does it mean that Mary saw Jesus but didn't perceive Him?

When are times in your life when you might see Jesus but not truly perceive Him?

Here's the beautiful, beautiful part of this story. Jesus didn't leave Mary where she was, seeing but not perceiving. He called her from the depths of blindness and opened her eyes with one word: her name.

Read John 20:16

Oh, what joy this verse brings! Jesus called Mary by name, and she recognized His voice! I get goosebumps every time I picture this scene. Jesus did not walk away, shrugging His shoulders at the fact that Mary allowed her emotions to blind her. The Good Shepherd called her by name.

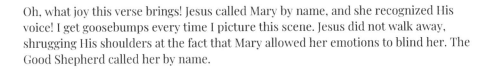

And she heard His voice and turned to Him.

What are other verses that talk about Jesus as our shepherd?

What is the significance of Mary recognizing Jesus once she heard Him call her by name?

What is comforting about the way Jesus responded to Mary?

Mary's response to Jesus calling her by name was immediate belief. She threw aside her doubts and fears and ran to her Savior. She could've been angry. She could've blamed Him for what she had to endure. Or she could've said enough is enough and walked away.

But she ran to Him. She embraced Him. She cried out to Him.

Will you do the same when He calls you by name?

What do you need to do to shed doubt and respond to Jesus' call as Mary did?

What distractions do you need to rid yourself of in order to hear Jesus call you by name?

Like Mary trying to fix the situation and search for Jesus' body herself, how do you try to control your earthly circumstances instead of listening for Jesus' voice? (Use top of next page for more space.)

Today's content was a bit longer than normal. Take time to pray through these questions and the verses you read. Think through and write out different ways you can listen for Jesus' voice. He has called you by name, just as He called Mary. He gently speaks to you, waiting for you to recognize His voice. How will you respond?

Reflection

Day 3

The Mission

The nightmare was over. Jesus was alive. Mary, with a cry of joy, fell at Jesus' feet in worship. We aren't sure exactly what Mary did, but we know from Jesus' words she clung to Him in some way. Whether she grasped His hands to find assurance of His life or kissed His feet in humble submission.

We do know Jesus had a mission for her, and He wanted to make sure Mary heard His words.

Read John 20:17–18

Jesus wanted to communicate to Mary that He wasn't staying on earth for good. That was not the purpose of His coming back to life. He also wanted her to understand He was not leaving at that very moment but would remain on earth for a little while longer. She had no reason to fear.

What was Mary's mission and why would this have been significant for a woman?

What part of this mission would have been difficult for Mary?

The earliest manuscripts and some other ancient witnesses do not contain these verses.

Read Mark 16:9–11

Why did God use the testimony of a woman to declare His resurrection?

Let's think even beyond the fact that Mary was a woman when it comes to sharing the testimony of Jesus' life. Jesus commanded her to go and tell. Which meant she had to go to the disciples and declare Jesus was alive. These were the men who had abandoned Jesus. Who had walked with Him for three years yet deserted Him in His time of need.

And Mary, a woman, was the one Jesus appeared to first. How nerve-wracking it must have been for Mary to have to share this news with these men!

We read how the disciples did not believe Mary at first. What must have been going through her mind and heart as she heard their unbelief of her words?

What do you fear most when telling others about Jesus?

How can you draw encouragement from Mary when it comes to bearing witness that Jesus is alive?

I'm guessing the unbelief of the disciples didn't dissuade Mary from what she knew to be true. She might have feared it was all a dream or a vision, but at the end of the day, she knew the truth. How encouraging this is! To know that everything was stacked against her, yet she stood her ground and shared the truth about Jesus!

No matter her circumstances, Mary remained faithful.

In the face of changing her entire life, serving Jesus as a woman in that culture, standing at the foot of the cross while Jesus died and now being the first to bear witness of His resurrection.

Was she perfect? Absolutely not. But she can teach us how to stand firm in our faith when everything else around us feels unstable.

Read Matthew 7:24–27

What rains did Mary experience? What enabled her to stand firm (yes, the answer should be more than "Jesus"!)?

How can you stand firm and obey Jesus' voice even when those around you doubt?

God used Mary in a way she probably never expected. She was a woman serving Jesus in a way that was difficult, yes, but also probably within her scope of talents. She most likely believed her role was to serve Jesus as He taught, and that's where it ended.

But God had something greater in mind for her. Her voice was the first one to bear witness that Jesus was alive. Not only was that an incredible gift for her to experience, but it also was a way God glorified His Name. The testimony of a woman would not have been trusted. So the fact that these men have told the story of Jesus' resurrection based on Mary's words means they believed her testimony. They wouldn't have given their lives for a lie.

Mary's testimony was the first obedience to the Great Commission. Can you even imagine Jesus placing that act of service in your hands? But if He trusted Mary to go and tell, He will trust all of us, too.

How does this aspect of Mary's story encourage you to remember God can use you in ways you might not even currently realize? Reflect on different ways God has used you when you didn't expect it. If you can't think of anything specific, pray through having a listening ear and obedient heart as God directs you into His service.

Reflection

Day 4

The Word of Our Testimony

*Y*esterday we ended talking about how God entrusts all of us with a mission. It's a simple mission, really. We all must go and tell.

And I believe we all truly want to change the world in God's Name. We all want Him to use us. But the problem we face is we don't understand how He'll use us. Or we fear maybe we've missed His calling. Maybe we were blinded by emotion or sin and just completely missed it.

Here's some truth, though:

None of us can ruin God's plans.

If Mary hadn't obeyed Jesus, He would've used someone else to proclaim the good news. But imagine what Mary would have missed out on if she hadn't!

On one hand, we don't understand how God will use us. But on the other hand, we believe we can't do whatever God has called us to do. Fear and doubt creep into play. We start wondering if the big dreams we had to make a difference for God are just too big. We could never actually accomplish that.

What dreams do you have for making a difference for God?

What steps have you taken to walk toward that dream?

When it comes to making a difference for God and being used by Him, we must remember this truth: Jesus doesn't need us, but He wants us. He will use us. But He doesn't expect us to change the world all at once.

Read 1 Peter 2:4–10

Why are you precious to God?

How does this passage encourage you and remind you God will use you?

We easily adapt a mindset that we must do grand things for God. But that's not what He's asked of us. What was Mary's mission? Go and tell the disciples. That didn't take special training. It didn't require very much at all from Mary. All it required was obedience.

Mary was able to set aside whatever self-doubt or fear she had as she obeyed. She must have struggled with the thought of, *Who am I to have this task?* For that is one of the enemy's goals. To make us believe our testimony is not right for the task at hand. Whether we believe it too boring or too shameful or too insignificant. Satan desires to shut us up because he knows the power of obeying Christ and sharing our testimony. He knows it will be his downfall.

Read Revelation 12:10–12

How was Satan triumphed over in these verses?

What does that tell you about the power of sharing your testimony?

What does sharing your testimony have to do with being used by God?

Sometimes it just starts with a small act of obedience. If you don't know how God will use you, start with prayer. Ask for wisdom and guidance and for God to shape you into a servant for Him. Then start watching and waiting. As you go throughout each day, watch for opportunities for God to use you.

For when you see those opportunities, all it takes is a "yes" from you. God doesn't need you, but He wants to use you.

Reflect below on any lies you believe that tell you your testimony is not worth sharing. Search the Bible for verses that combat those lies with truth. Then pray through how God can use you this week.

Reflection

Day 5

A Changed Life

*W*ant to know something kind of sad? We don't know anything else about Mary. Her name is not mentioned after she proclaimed Christ as alive. But that's not to say she disappeared from the lives of Jesus' followers. We know her too well by now to think she would have gone anywhere.

Read Acts 1:1–14

What must Jesus' followers—the disciples and the women always by His side—have been feeling during this time following Jesus' ascension?

What danger were they all most likely in during this time?

Some have researched whether or not she went to Ephesus to proclaim Jesus as they began a new church there. Others wonder if the Romans removed her from Jerusalem in attempts to snuff out Jesus' followers. And then there's the question of whether or not she married John, the disciple of Jesus, although there's really no evidence to support this.

How do you think they got through these days? (Use top of next page for more space as needed.)

Mary must have felt like this time was the end of an era. Do you know that feeling? When something wonderful has happened, and you're not sure how to go on now that the wonderful is no longer your current reality?

One thing we know for sure: These men and women knew the importance of prayer. Acts tells us they were in constant prayer, which sounds overwhelming. But it tells us just how much they relied upon God for their daily needs—physical, emotional and spiritual needs, no doubt.

And, just as Jesus promised, their prayers were met with the Holy Spirit.

Whether or not Mary was present for that dramatic moment of receiving the Holy Spirit, it's certain she would never be the same again. She was healed from her demons, had seen miracles transpire and learned at the feet of God in human flesh. Now, she received the Holy Spirit as a seal promising she would forever and always belong to her Savior.

But what now? Mary was most likely filled with questions and doubts about how she was to carry on now that Jesus was no longer among them. But God never ends a journey without the next step in mind.

What might have been the hardest aspect of this new beginning for Mary?

Why do you think her testimony would have been important as the Church began to take shape?

In what ways would Mary have had to trust Jesus differently now that He was taken back to heaven?

When I think about how Mary has made a difference in this world, I think that she probably wasn't setting out to do so. She simply loved Jesus and knew she wanted to follow Him with everything she had. He had changed her life, and she couldn't bear to live the way she had been living before He freed her.

We want so badly to make a difference for God. But what if, like Mary, we simply focused on loving Him in every way we know how? What if we shared our testimony to anyone and everyone who would listen? What if we took each day at a time, walking in obedience and listening for Jesus' voice calling us by name?

That's what Mary did. And want to know something crazy and wonderful? We have the same power within us as Mary had. We have the Holy Spirit guiding us and enabling us to make a difference in all the little ways we can each day.

Read Romans 8:1–11 (or the whole chapter for some amazing encouragement!)

Why can we have confidence that we truly can make a difference for God?

What does it look like to have our minds set on what the Spirit desires?

How does that change the way we live for God?

We've come to the end of our time together. I hope you have come to love Mary and find great encouragement from her. She wasn't a woman to place up on a pedestal for her perfection or out-of-this-world strength. She was human, like you and me. She sinned. She allowed her emotions to take over truth. She doubted. But we can find encouragement because through it all, she remained faithful to her Savior. It's my prayer we will all walk in such faithfulness daily. That we will all hear the voice of Jesus and respond with excited obedience. But whatever you do, don't close the pages of this study and go back to living life the way you always have. Allow Mary's life to strengthen you. Learn from her mistakes and her accomplishments and her faithfulness. And know, above all else, that Jesus loves you enough to call you by name.

How has Jesus changed your life?

What are ways your routine can change based on what Jesus did for you and then also based on what you've learned about Mary? Spend some time in reflection, praying and writing through what you've learned this past month.

Reflection

Jesus loves
you enough
to call you
by name

Bibliography

1. Shanks, Hershel. "Exclusive! Major New Excavation Planned for Mary Magdalene's Hometown." Biblical Archaeology Review, Biblical Archaeology Society, Sept./Oct. 2007, http://www.basarchive.org/sample/bswbBrowse.asp? PubID=BSBA&Volume=33&Issue=5&ArticleID=10. Accessed 31 August 2017 par. 1, 6, 7
2. Chilton Bruce. Mary Magdalene A Biography. Doubleday, 2005. pp. 4-5
3. Lucas, Dorothy J., MD, MPH, D.MIN. A History of Women in Religion. Xulon Press, 2010. p. 20
4. Carson, D. A., et al. The Expositor's Bible Commentary. Edited by Frank E. Gaebelein, vol. 8, The Zondervan Corporation, 1984. p. 905
5. Carson, p. 584
6. Cocherell, B.L. "THE SPICES AND THE VISITS TO CHRIST'S TOMB." Bibleresearch.org. 2 June 2015. Access date: August 22, 2017. http://www.bibleresearch.org/observancebook5/b5w79.html par. 7
7. Tenney, Merrill C., Longenecker, Richard N. The Expositor's Bible Commentary. Edited by Frank E. Gaebelein, vol. 9, The Zondervan Corporation, 1981. p. 190

More from Emily:

Learn more about each eBook on tounearth.com

Prayers for Your Ordinary

Discover God in the midst of your ordinary through this 10-day prayer devotional. Each day has normal, everyday experiences we face with prayer prompts to guide you in seeing God at work. Read the Scripture provided to help you get started in your prayer time as you discover where your routine meets God's extraordinary.

Rekindled

For the heart needing a gentle reminder of how to find joy in Christ. This one-week devotional is designed to help you gain excitement and joy back into your faith using Scripture and questions to stir your heart. Because sometimes we need a little rekindling to remind us of our passion for Jesus.

The Invitation

We all long to invite Jesus into our routines, especially around the season of autumn when hospitality is in the air. This one-week devotional is designed to help you invite God into your daily moments using Scripture and reflection questions.

Made in the USA
Middletown, DE
01 December 2019

Prostitute. Jesus' mistress. Shameful. Sin-filled past.
Jesus called her by name.
And He calls you by name, too...

When we hear the name Mary Magdalene, ideas of promiscuity and sinful legacies often march across our thoughts. But when we take a deeper look into this woman's history, we find her struggles and victories were not that different from our own. "He Calls Us by Name" uniquely explores Mary Magdalene's life and reclaims her honor using Scripture as well as historical facts in order to not only discover the truth of her story, but also realize the deep love Jesus has for us and the freedom we can find in Him when He calls us by name.

Join me in opening these pages to Mary's past as we learn how to change our future and even our present. Each week of this study includes five days of Scripture to read, questions to answer and thoughts upon which to reflect. You'll read through guided study and then pick up your pen as you allow the Holy Spirit to direct your thoughts as you write out answers and reflection and prayers.

Are you ready? Ready to hear Jesus call you by name and take a stand for your faith? Open "He Calls Us by Name" and learn how one woman's story can challenge and encourage us all to be used by God and know our worth as we serve Him and love Him daily. It's not about doing something exceptional. It's about remaining faithful.

Emily Saxe is founder and managing editor of To Unearth, a devotional-based website helping people see God at work in their ordinary. Her heart and pen are drawn to stories of faith as she helps people share how God is working in their lives. Emily lives in Indiana with her husband where she works full-time as a freelance writer and editor.

 To Unearth | Helping you find the exceptional in your ordinary
tounearth.com
emilysaxewrites.com

ISBN 9781734258202

9 781734 258202